Windows 10 May 2019 10 Update

The Ultimate guide for Fixing Windows 10 update problems

With 101

Tips& tricks

David H. Kevin

either electronic means or in printed format. The recording of this strictly prohibited and the document is not allowed unless with written permission from the publisher. All rights reserved.

The information provided herein is stated to be truthful and consistent, in that any liability, in terms of inattention or otherwise, by any use or abuse of any policies, processes, or directions contained within is the solitary and utter responsibility of the recipient reader. Under no circumstances will any legal the publisher for any reparation, damages, or monetary loss due to the information herein, either directly or indirectly.

IBSN: 9781694400895

Printed in the United States of America

Graw-Hill Publishing House

2 Penn Plaza,

NY 10121

New York

USA

Dedication

To my parents, patty jean, Henry Kevin, and my Loving wife Diana, who is a constant source of Encouragement, love and positive reinforcement.

Contents

Windows 10 May 2019 Update

The Ultimate Guide For Fixing Windows 10 May 2019 Update Problems

with 101 Tips & Tricks

David H. Kevin

CHAPTER ONE

Introduction

I want to thank you and congratulate you for downloading the book, "Windows 10 May 2019 update- the Ultimate guide, for fixing Windows 10 update problems".

This book contains proven steps, strategies, tips and tricks on How to master Windows 10 within 24 hours".

Thanks again for downloading this book, I hope you enjoy it!

With the Windows 10 May 2019 Update, Windows 10 is more protected, reliable and efficient than ever, offering essential features that will truly save you time and frustration as well as keep your PC protected. Of course, there's constantly room for improvement, but Windows 10 is now better than ever before and still continues to develop with a slide of constant updates.

Windows 10

Windows 10 has improved with;

✓ *Start menu enhancements*

✓ *Action Center, Cortana is useful*

- ✓   *Edge continues to improve*

- ✓   *Windows Hello faster, easier*

- ✓   *Timeline genuinely useful*

But despite it's great improvement, Windows 10 encounter some glitches

- ✓   *OneDrive needs work*

- ✓   *Improvements also cause some problem*

- ✓   *Some changes are incomplete*

Anybody that's tracked Windows 10 very closely already knows that Microsoft isn't releasing new versions of Windows like it used to. Instead of giving its operating system (OS) an overhaul every few years, Microsoft made Windows 10, released as a platform that gets minor yet tangible semi-annual free updates.

Windows 10 gets Arch Linux, one of the trickiest OS around

This innovative approach is working out impeccably. Windows 10 has taken Windows 7's mantle as the most popular OS, even exceeding 900 million users (and getting closer to that one billion mark). This is appreciations in large part to the recurrent updates, the most recent of which is the Windows 10 May 2019

Update.

Nevertheless, Windows 10 is much more than just the sum of its updates. Presently, the OS has different versions, each of which is specifically created for different hardware and users. For instance, Windows 10 S Mode locks down the OS, with only Microsoft Store apps allowed to be installed. It's obstructive, to be sure, but it's also the best option for low-end hardware and dummies users.

Another example is Windows 10 Lite, which may be Microsoft's initial effort to compete with the best Chromebooks and the ChromeOS. With Microsoft perhaps announcing new hardware at their

October 2 event, we could see this alleged lightweight OS making at appearance soon.

On top of that, there are rumblings that Microsoft is putting together an even more fundamentals version of the OS – Windows 10 Lean Mode – as well as gossips of Windows 10 for foldable devices.

System Requirements

All of these spin-offs and updates have assisted Windows 10 to be the most modern OS out there – bringing in new features and support that go far beyond the traditional computer.

If this sounds like it's up your lane, and you want to pick up a Windows 10 license for your computer, you can get the Home Edition for $140 (£119, and Windows 10 Pro for $200. Downloads of Windows 10 Home Edition can be found available for just $100 in the US, if you look hard enough.

If you haven't flown on the Windows 10 bandwagon yet, in this piece, we'll help you decide if it is worth your time, money and hard drive space. But first, let's dive into all the detailed of the Windows 10 May 2019 Update.

With the Windows 10 May 2019 Update release comes some new impressive features and improvements — as well as minor but still welcome additions — to make your desktop environment even secure as well as more efficient, giving users an experience that's even more unified.

There are couple of features that Microsoft is removing out and a handful that Microsoft may completely take out from a future update. But, what's worth noting here are the best new features of this latest update.

Windows 10 Sandbox

We get it, and Microsoft gets it as well. When running a new .exe file from the web, especially if it's not from a renowned software company, there's always some risk. Users who are more cautious about their security would generally use a virtual machine so as to avert harm to their PC if the file happens to be infected or corrupt. The billions of users who just have no idea how to set up this virtual machine, though, would maybe just take the risk.

With the Windows 10 May 2019 Update, they won't need to use a virtual machine any longer. Everybody can simply take advantage of this well-designed Windows Sandbox feature, as it basically creates a temporary and disposable desktop background in which they can run that .exe file and test the app they're installing. Doing so isolates it — and should in case any potential harm that comes with it. Bear in mind still that Windows Sandbox is only available in Windows 10 Pro and Windows 10 Enterprise

CHAPTER TWO

Windows 10 May update problems

The Windows 10 May 2019 Update launched on May 22, and Microsoft has done a great effort to make sure that this latest major update to Windows 10 is not afflicted by the same level of hitches that the October 2018 Update suffered, unfortunely, there have been already some Windows 10 May 2019 Update identified problems spotted.

So, we've composed up all the Windows 10 May 2019 Update problems and fixes in this guide, so you don't have to search the internet if your windows 10 PC isn't behaving well.

How to download and install the Windows 10 May 2019 Update right now

If you need to install the update now, select Start > Settings > Update & Security > Windows Update, then select Check for updates. ...

If your version 1903 isn't offered automatically over Check for updates, but you can get it manually through the Update Assistant.

Windows 10 May 2019 Update name

Before as the 'Windows 10 April 2019

Update', Microsoft revised new that to 'May 2019', and publicly it's referred to as 'Windows 10 version 1903' or by its codename Windows 19H1.

How to do Windows 10 may update

How to download Windows 10 May 2019 Update using Windows Update

1. Open Settings.

2. Click Update & Security.

3. Click Windows Update.

4. Click on the Check for updates button.

5. Click the Download and install now button, in the Feature Update to Windows 10, version 1903 section.

The latest version of Windows in 2019

On 13, November, 2018, re-released the Windows 10 October Update (version 1809), Windows Server 2019, and Windows Server, version 1809. We cheer you to wait until the feature update is offered to your device automatically.

The new features in Windows Server 2019?

1. The new Storage Spaces Direct

2. De-duplication and compression for ReFS volumes.

3. Native support for persistent memory space.

4. Nested resiliency for two-node hyper-

converged infrastructure at the edge.

5. Two-server clusters by means of a USB flash drive as a witness.

6. Windows Admin Center support.

7. Performance history.

8. Scale up to 4 PB / cluster.

How to fix Cortana high CPU usage in Windows 10 May 2019 Update

Microsoft released the Windows 10 KB4512941 update for the Windows 10 May 2019 Update, and whereas the update has brought a number of fixes, it has also introduced some problem where some users are seeing extremely high CPU usage after installing the update –

which is caused by Cortana, Microsoft's voice assistant.

To fix this issue, open the Registry by pressing Windows + R on your keyboard and type in 'regedit'.

Open up 'HKEY_CURRENT_USER' then browse to \Software\Microsoft\Windows\CurrentVersion\Search.

There, you'll discover a registry entry called 'BingSearch Enabled'. Select it, and then set the 'Reg Value' to 0.

This will automatically stop local search queries you perform on your computer being sent to Bing, Microsoft's search engine, which appears like the main cause of the high CPU usage issue.

You can similarly fix the issue by uninstalling the May 2019 update by opening up Settings, clicking 'Update & Security', click on 'View update history'. Click 'Uninstall updates' then select the KB4512941 update and then click 'Uninstall'.

Check Microsoft's list box of known Windows 10 May 2019 Update issues

Not like October, 2018 Windows 10 Updates, Microsoft has newly created a webpage where you can view the current

Windows 10 May 2019 problems, along with details information on the how to fix them.

Make sure you check the web page to see if the problems you are experiencing is known to Microsoft, and whatever the steps you need to take to fix it.

Here are the list of problems Microsoft knows about with Windows 10 May 2019 Update and exactly how to fix them:

Your Bluetooth devices not working with Windows 10 May 2019 Update

If you've establish that your Bluetooth

device is no longer correctly working with your Windows 10 May 2019 Update, at that point a recent security update for the Windows 10 May 2019 Update (and other versions of Windows) is expected to be the cause of the problem.

The patch is intended at older Bluetooth devices that pose security risks. According to the Microsoft company: " You may experience issues pairing, connecting or using certain Bluetooth devices after installing security updates released June 2019. These security updates report a security susceptibility by intentionally preventing connections from Windows to unsecure Bluetooth devices."

So it's essentially designed to stop certain Bluetooth devices connecting to your computer. To fix this issue, you should either consider changing to a latest — and more secure — Bluetooth device, or contact the maker of your Bluetooth device to see if there is recent update for the device.

If you want to continue using the Bluetooth device, then you'll need to roll back your Windows 10 May 2019 Update computer to before the security update was installed. Though, we don't recommend this.

Display of brightness may not respond to adjustments

Some Intel display drivers were mismatched with the Windows 10 May 2019 May Update, which means you could not change the brightness of your screen display.

This can be fixed with the KB4505057 patch, which will be installed automatically.

Audio not properly working with Dolby Atmos headphones and home theater in May 2019 Update

A Windows 10 May 2019 Update that some people were experience meant that some Dolby Atmos sound systems did not work properly.

This can be fixed with the KB4505057 patch, which will be installed automatically.

Duplicate folders and documents display in user profile directory

An error in the May 2019 Update where if some folders (e.g. Desktop, Documents, or Pictures folders) are redirected, an empty folder with same name might be created.

This has already been fixed with the KB4505057 patch, which will be installed automatically.

AMD RAID driver incompatibility in windows 10

Installation process could stop when trying to install Windows 10 May 2019 Update on your computers that run certain versions of AMD RAID drivers.

This has also been fixed with the KB4505057 patch, which will be installed automatically.

Error in trying to install Windows 10 May 2019 Update with external USB or memory card attached

Computers with an external USB device or SD memory card attached may get error: "This computer can't be upgraded to Windows 10."

This has also been fixed with the KB4505057 patch, which will be installed automatically.

Unable to connect or discover Bluetooth devices in Windows 10 May 2019 Update

Microsoft has recognized compatibility issues with certain versions of Realtek and Qualcomm Bluetooth radio drivers.

This has been fixed with the

KB4505057 patch, which will be installed automatically.

Night light settings do not apply in certain cases

Microsoft has recognized some scenarios where night light settings may completely stop working.

This has been fixed with the KB4505057 patch, which will be installed automatically.

Intel Audio displays an intcdaud.sys notification

Microsoft and Intel have acknowledged an issue with a range of Intel Display

Audio device drivers that may cause in battery drain.

This has been fixed with the KB4505057 patch, which will be installed automatically.

Cannot launch Camera app in Windows 10 May 2019 Update

Microsoft and Intel have acknowledged an issue upsetting Intel RealSense SR300 or Intel RealSense S200 camera apps.

This has been fixed with the KB4505057 patch, which will be automatically installed.

Intermittent loss of computer Wi-Fi

connectivity

Some older computers may experience loss of Wi-Fi connectivity due to an outdated Qualcomm driver.

This has been fixed with the KB4505057 patch, which will be automatically installed.

Direct3D applications and games may fail to enter full-screen mode on rotated displays

Some Direct3D (D3D) applications and games may not to enter full-screen mode on rotated displays.

This has been fixed with the KB4505057 patch, which will be

automatically installed.

Older types of BattlEye anti-cheat software are incompatible with Windows 10 May 2019 Update

Microsoft and BattlEye have recognized a compatibility issue with some games that use older versions of BattlEye anti-cheat software.

This has been fixed with the KB4505057 patch, which will be automatically installed.

Missing some features after installing the Windows 10 May 2019 Update

Have you observed that some features you used to rely on have missing after installing the Windows 10 May 2019 Update?

Unfortunately, this isn't a virus, but rather a deliberate move by Microsoft to clean up Windows 10 and remove old and hardly used features. You can check out the list of the features Microsoft has dropped from Windows 10 May 2019 Update to see which ones have been cut.

How to fix Windows 10 May 2019 Update installation problems

If you're run into problems installing Windows 10 May 2019 Update via Windows 10's update tool, don't worry. Windows 10 has a built-in troubleshooter that can support and identify any problems. This can reset the Windows Update app, which also can help kickstart the installation.

To do this, click on Start menu, then click the cog icon on the left, which will open up the Settings window. Click 'Update and Security' then 'Troubleshoot'. Click 'Windows Update' then 'Run the troubleshooter' and follow the instructions, and click 'Apply this fix' if the troubleshooter finds a solution.

Windows 10 May 2019 Update problems free up disk space

As with earlier updates for Windows 10,

the May 2019 Update requires a specific amount of hard drive space to successfully download and install. If the main hard drive (where Windows 10 is installed, usually the C: drive), is nearly full, then you'll come across difficulties when trying to install Windows 10 May 2019 Update.

The May 2019 Update needs 16GB of free space for the 32-bit version, while the 64-bit version required 20GB on the hard drive where Windows 10 is installed.

The first thing to do if the Windows 10 May 2019 Update install fails is to check your drive space in Windows

Explorer. If it is running out of space, typing in "Disk Clean-up" in the search box on the taskbar and select the system disk (regularly the C: drive).

Click 'OK' then choice the tick boxes of the files you want to delete. These should be safe to remove, remember that you can't recover them once they're gone. You'll be told how much space you'll save. Click 'OK' then 'Delete files' to remove the files. If you need to create more space, click 'Clean up system files'.

As soon as that's done, try downloading and installing the Windows 10 May 2019 update again.

Windows 10 May 2019 Update install displays 0x80190001, 0x80073712, or 0x80245006 errors

If you get an error message after installing the Windows 10 May 2019 Update, and it displays a string of numbers like 0x80190001, 0x80073712, or 0x80245006 then it may well mean that your computer needs more disk space.

To fix this problem,

Open Settings, go to System > Storage, at that point where it says 'Storage sense', click 'Free up space now'.

Select what you like to remove - and make

sure 'Temporary Windows 10 installation files' and 'Windows Setup temporary files' are both selected. Then click 'Remove files'.

Then, open up the Windows Update app and select 'Check for updates' to try installing again.

Anti-virus software in windows 10 is disable

Antivirus software without doubt is helpful to have, but it can occasionally cause problems when installing the Windows 10 May 2019 Update.

If you have installed antivirus software,

try disabling it before trying to install the Windows 10 May 2019 Update, as that may probably fix the problem. You must enable it and use it normally once the installation has completed.

You may need to uninstall the software temporarily. But make sure that you reinstall it once the update installs successfully.

Update Reset

If you are experiencing problems when trying to install the Windows 10 May 2019 Update, then you need to reset the update service and try again.

To do this, open the Command Prompt

by typing in 'CMD' into the search bar and then right-clicking on 'Command Prompt'. Select 'Run as administrator'.

Fix the Windows 10 May 2019 Update using the command prompt

Subsequently, restart your computer and try installing the May 2019 Update again.

Update Assistant gets jammed when downloading Windows 10 May 2019 Update

Here's how to fix the problem where the Update Assistant gets jammed and becomes unresponsive when downloading the Windows 10 May 2019 Update.

Firstly, reboot your computer, then try running the Update Assistant once again. If that still doesn't work, either unplug your computer from the network tangibly, or disable the connection by typing in 'network adapter' into the search box in the taskbar.

Click 'Change network adapter option', and in the window that display click 'Change adapter options'.

Right-click on your network adapter, select 'Disable'. This turns of the internet connection to your computer. Count to 20 seconds, then right-click it again and select

'Enable'.

How to fix May 2019 Update 0x800F0922 error

If the Windows 10 May 2019 Update fails with 0x800F0922 error, this may be as result of an active VPN connection that's interfering with Windows 10 contacting the update servers. To fix this problem, disconnect from the VPN server and try once more.

The VPN stand for (Virtual Private Network) is, then it means you probably don't have a connection, but check with your IT administrator. This error can occur if the System Reserved partition on your hard drive is full or not big enough. Any third party software tool can help you to resize your partition.

Install the Windows 10 May 2019 Update via USB

If you're having trouble downloading and installing the Windows 10 May 2019 Update, you should try installing it from your USB drive.

Here, you need a blank DVD or a USB stick to add to the installation files, with at least 5 Gigabytes of spare space. If you don't get a spare drive, then check out our list of the best USB flash drives 2019.

Download and install it, then open it up and click on agree to the license terms. On the "What do you want to do?" screen, then click "Create installation media for another computer", then select 'Next'. Select the language, edition and either 32-bit or 64-bit, then select 'USB flash drive' or ISO file', depending on whether you're installing from a USB or from a DVD (choice ISO for the latter).

Microsoft has made the Windows 10 May 2019 Update ISO files available for download, though, the links expired after 24 hours.

But, Ittechtics.com has re-hosted the ISO files. If you indeed want to download the

ISO files, you can download it from there, however we'd always advice download ISO files from the Microsoft.

How to fix Windows 10 May 2019 Update Media Creation Tool issues

The Media Creation Tool is a manageable app made by Microsoft that lets you to install the Windows 10 May 2019 Update using a USB drive or DVD. Still, some people have encountered problems when using it.

If the Media Creation Tool becomes stuck when you're trying to download the Windows 10 May 2019 Update files, try closing and reopening the Media Creation

Tool app. When the app has downloaded the files, quickly disconnect your computer from the network (either remove the Ethernet cable or turn off your Wi-Fi adapter).

The installation ought to continue (without checking the internet for more files) and when it's complete you can reconnect to the internet. Lastly, open up Windows Update (Settings > Update & Security > Windows Update) and then click 'Check for Updates' to download the final files.

Some people are getting a 'DynamicUpdate' error message when using the Media Creation Tool. To fix this problem, open File Explorer and go to C:\$Windows.~WS\Sources\Windows\sources.

You would see an app called Setupprep.exe. Double-click it to launch the update program.

How to fix corrupted ISO issues with Windows 10 May 2019 Update

If you're trying to install the Windows 10 May 2019 Update using an ISO file, and you've experienced an error numbered 0x8007025D - 0x2000C, then this may indicate that the Windows 10 May 2019 Update might be corrupted.

If this occurs, try downloading the ISO file once again, then run the Media Creation Tool again to create a bootable USB or DVD and try again.

How to fix issues that stop Windows 10 May 2019 Update from finishing the install

There's nothing more provoking than seeing an update seemingly install without an issues, and then getting an error message at the last moment.

A lot of people are reporting that they're seeing 'Error: We couldn't complete the updates. Undoing changes. Don't turn off your PC' and 'Error: Failure configuring

Windows Updates. Reverting changes' messages, which stop Windows 10 May 2019 Update from finishing the install process.

You can also check to see what went wrong by go to Settings>Update and Security>Windows Update and clicking 'Update history'.

This would show you if there any problems that were encountered. Take a note of these, then search the internet for a solution.

Repair your hard drive in Windows 10 May 2019 Update

If Windows 10 May 2019 Update is struggling to install, you can check hard drive for errors. To do this, you just need to use the CHKDSK command in the command prompt.

Type "command prompt" into the search box in taskbar, right-click "Command Prompt" and then select "Run as administrator".

When window opens type in the following, then press Enter on your keyboard:

chkdsk/f c:

You may be asked to press Y or Enter on your keyboard to confirm the check. Just allow it to run, and if any errors are found, follow the instructions to fix it.

How to uninstall Windows 10 May 2019 Update

If you're still facing a problems with the Windows 10 May 2019 Update, or you don't like the changes Microsoft has made, then you can instantly uninstall the May 2019 Update and revert to a former version of Windows.

We wouldn't really advise doing this, as you might miss out on future security updates from Microsoft, but if you would prefer to go back until all the bugs and issues with the Windows 10 May 2019

Update has been generally fixed, then follow these steps.

Go to Settings > Update and security > Recovery and click on 'Get started' under where it says 'Go back to the previous version of Windows 10'.

A new window will appear requesting you why you want to revert to a previous version. Answer the question (this will helps Microsoft improve future versions of Windows), then click 'No, thanks' from the next window. This is where it asks you if you like to check for any updates.

Click 'Next' on the window that follows, then 'Next' again, ensure you have your

Windows log in details handy. Lastly, click 'Go back to earlier build' and the Windows 10 May 2019 Update will automatically uninstall.

If you wait for more than 10 days to uninstall the Windows 10 May 2019 Update, you might find the option is gone. Unfortunately, the only way to uninstall the May 2019 Update after that is to execute a fresh install of Windows 10 using an ISO file of an older version.

CHAPTER THREE

How fix it, May 2019 Updates Problems

Experiencing problems with the latest version of Windows 10 you just can't figure out? In this chapter you should be able to learn how to identify Windows 10 2019 update problems and how to fix them!

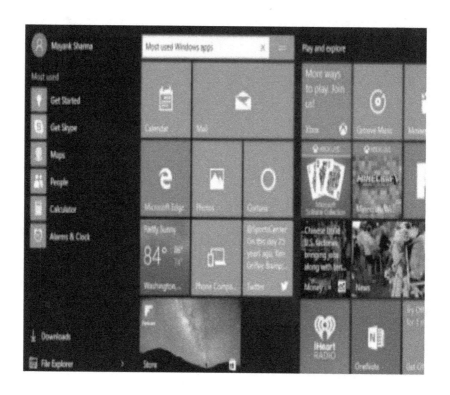

Removing built-in apps

The Windows 10 May 2019 Update is including more on the list of built-in apps you can get rid of, freeing up storage space – or at the very least, letting you cuddle out every ounce of extra space you can get, *if you don't want to spend more money for a bigger hard drive or solid state drive.*

The apps added to the roster comprise of Mail and Calendar, Movies & TV, Groove Music, Calculator, Paint 3D and 3D Viewer.

Decoupling Cortana and search

Microsoft Search has a long way to go, but thanks to the Windows 10 May 2019 Update, at least you won't have to suffer over Cortana when you're doing a search in the Windows 10 taskbar, if you're not a great fan of the feature. This allow you perform text searches for your most frequently used apps, files and documents, and most recent activities distinctly from voice queries, giving you the option to select the approach you're prefer and to stick with it.

New kaomoji face characters

Emoji admirers will be happy to know that the Windows 10 May 2019 Update also comes with a a bit of adorable kaomoji face characters, accessible through the emoji shortcut, so that Windows 10 users won't have to make them manually when sending cute messages to their family and friends.

Pausing updates

Microsoft is giving control back to its

esteems users, as far as its updates are concerned. Windows 10 users no longer have to sit through overlong time on updates, especially if their attention is needed somewhere else, as well as choose when and what they want to update. With the Windows 10 May 2019 Update, users can now pause updates at ant time, choose when to install the new update and even opt out of it, if they want to.

Moreover, Microsoft is now setting aside roughly 7Gigabytes of storage space specifically for Windows Updates. This mean, Windows 10 users will no longer have to scramble to free up storage in order to get the most new updates.

Less cluttered Start Menu

One of the most provoking aspects — not that there's a lot — about Windows 10 in general is the amount of clutter it has. Good thing Microsoft is cleaning up its act, at least when it comes to its Start Menu. With this update, all the bloatware will be assembled in one section, essentially cutting down the number of pinned apps you'll see in the Start Menu and giving it a cleaner appearance.

On the weakness, this new menu design is only be available to new user accounts only and newly set up Windows 10 computers. At least with this update.

Minor changes in windows 10 2019 update

Apart from these six major changes, the Windows 10 May 2019 Update boasts minor ones that users might also appreciate. That includes a new brightness slider, better Windows Mixed Reality VR support, a passwordless Microsoft Account and Windows 10 login etc.

CHAPTER FOUR

Windows 10 Quick Guide

The Start menu is one of the fastest ways to access files, folders, apps, settings and more. With the new start menu in Windows 10, you can simply access all of the windows menu much faster than in Windows 7.

When login for the first time, you will notice in the bottom right a small Windows icon.

Clicking on the Windows icon will convey the new start menu as shown below:

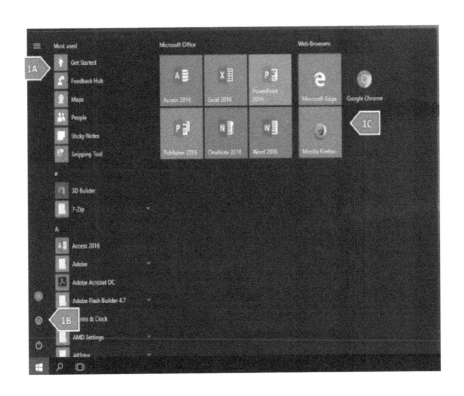

1A – Apps and Programs installed on the device will be found in this list. This list is the replacement to "All Applications" in Windows 7.

1B – Log off, settings, and shutdown buttons.

1C – These are the most frequently used programs on Windows, and have been made manageable in the tile menu for all users.

b. Logging Off or Shutting Down

There is a new location to log off, switch users, shut down, restart and more. To get these options, press the icons on the left-bottom side of the Start Menu. (You can Right Click the start menu and choice these options)

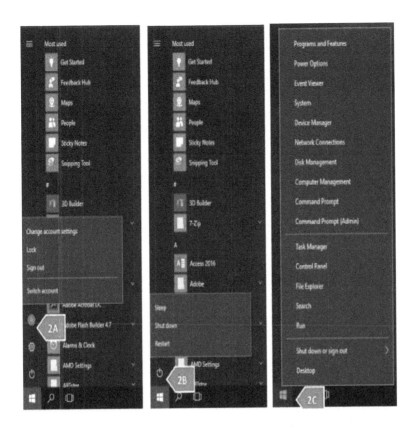

2A – The small PROFILE icon at the top shows your user account. Use this icon to lock the computer, sign out of the computer or to switch between users.

2B – The bottom POWER icon lets you to put the PC to sleep, shut it down and restart

2C – Right clicking the windows 10 icon brings up a quick list of quick-access programs and files. |

Navigating with Start Menu in windows 10

Using the START MENU is the quickest way to find files, folders, apps or programs in Windows 10.

To start searching press any of the Windows button, or the Search icon next to the windows icon on the bottom Task Bar.

When you click on one of the icons, start typing and your search results will display as you type. You can use the icons that show up as you type to narrow the search for exactly what type of item you are looking for.

Customization

User Picture

In Windows 10 you can be able to set a user picture that only you can see when you're logged in. Several people like to set this. To accomplish this feat, you start by pressing START and clicking the user icon, once you click this icon press Change

Account Settings."

On the subsequent screen you will have two options to create your picture, Camera

or Browse for One. If you are on a laptop, or have a webcam you can also use the camera, or else browse for one.

Looks great!

Color Theme and Wallpapers

With Windows 10 you can also customize the colors and wallpaper of how Windows is presented. To quickly do this, right click on the desktop in an empty space and select Personalize.

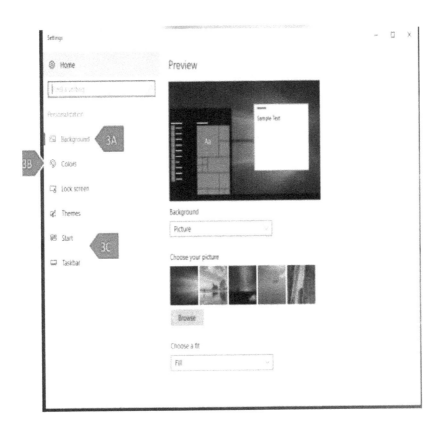

On this new screen for Personalization you will get the option to change your wallpaper. Clicking "browse" will allow you to change it to whatsoever image you want.

3A – In the background menu you can

change your background image.

3B – In the colors menu you can change the accent color and theme of the any apps. (light or dark)

3C – With the start and taskbar settings you can show or hide different menu options and change how you want them to appear.

As soon as you change the background and color you will see a preview of the changes and how they will look.

That's Perfect.

The Taskbar

The Taskbar is where all the opened and pinned programs appear in your desktop. Users can add programs to the task bar for better workflow as needed.

To add items to your taskbar, you can drag and drop items to it, or right clicking an icon and pressing "Add to Taskbar"

Right clicking in the Start Menu and hovering over MORE gives you an option to Pin to Taskbar.

Right clicking an open program in the taskbar provides a similar prompt to Pin to Taskbar

The coolest way to make other changes is to right click the taskbar in any open area that does not have an application open and press "settings". You can get to the taskbar settings by going through the Start Menu introduction steps.

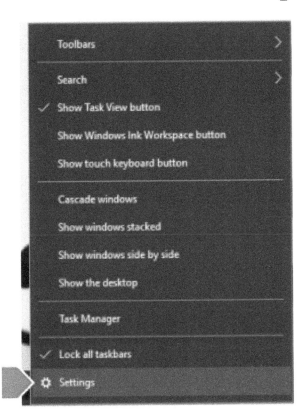

On the next screen you will discover options to modify the taskbar, including how the taskbar appears in size, how

icons appear and how multiple displays use the taskbar.

The *multiple display settings allow a single taskbar (similar to Windows 7) or multiple taskbars with the icons appearing on both displays.*

Feel free to try these experiment with all the settings to find the best layout that fits *what you want.*

Resetting Your Password in Windows

Resetting passwords can only be done using college maintained machine on campus. (Flagstaff and Page campuses)

a. Resetting with CTRL+ALT+DEL

On your keyboard, press CTRL+ALT +DEL on the keyboard.

✓ *On the new screen press "Change a password"*

✓ *On the new screen it have 4 fields*

✓ *Do not change the username field, leave it as "David\Come"*

✓ *Input your current password in the "Old Password" box*

✓ *Input what you need as a new password to be in the New Password and Confirm Password boxes*

✓ *Press Enter or press the small arrow next to the Confirm Password*

CHAPTER FIVE

101 tips and tricks of Windows 10

Windows 10 is packed with new and updated features for streamlining all your computing jobs. The new release cartels the familiarity of Windows 7 and the functionality of Windows 8.

Although you can also use some features to increase your productivity instinctively, others aren't so upcoming and require a trip down the menus and settings before they make your life easier.

We've compiled some of the Windows 10 tips and tricks by grouping the tips into sets, so it's now even easier to find the best Windows 10 tips for your immediate needs.

In this chapter we'll take you through Windows' nooks and crannies and help you twist your Windows installation in a variety of ways to suit your style of working and life style.

Using the tips and tricks, you'll be able to save some time off of tasks that need to be done regularly and streamline your navigation around the system. We'll also learn tips to help twist the new features centered on your preferences, enabling you to use your new installation properly.

Also make sure you check out other book from the author on how to use Windows 10 to make sure you get the most out of the new beast.

1. Using Custom Install

When you're setting up Windows 10 on a new computer, make sure you select the Custom install option as an alternative of the default Express install. It's more complex but allows you modify vital aspects of your installation such as the privacy settings.

2. How to remove old files after installing Windows 10

If you have no plans of reverting to the previous version of Windows, you can save disk space by getting clear of the old OS files. Go to Control Panel > System and Security > Administrative Tools > Disk Clean-up and then toggle the 'Previous Windows installations' box in the list.

3. Sign out of Windows 10

The Power menu in the Start menu merely includes options to Shut down and Restart the PC. To sign in as another user bring up the Start menu and click on your name shown at the top. This brings up a menu which includes the Sign out option

4. New Action Center of windows 10

Windows 10 contains a new Action Center that keeps track of all notifications from the system. Click on the text bubble icon in the system tray and the panel runs out from the right-hand side of the screen.

5. New snap keyboard shortcuts

Keyboard warriors can save your time and snap windows without using the mouse. Use the Win key + Arrow key to snap to one of the four screen corners of your PC and double-up commands to reach the quadrants. For instance, pressing Win + Right Arrow, then Win +Up Arrow homes the current window in the top-right corner.

6. Make Windows 10 touch-friendly

If your computer has a touch screen compatibility, you can manually enable Windows 10's touch-friendly Continuum interface to operate Windows in a tablet mode.

Go to Start > Settings > System > Tablet Mode to manually alter its activities.

7. Disable WiFi Sense in Windows 10

If you're worried about Wi-Fi Sense's security implications you can disable it by heading to Start > Settings > Network and Internet > Wi-Fi > Manage Wi-Fi settings. Just disable all options and ask Windows 10 to forget every Wi-Fi networks you've signed into in the past.

8. How to Customize Privacy settings

To take charge of general and app-specific privacy options Go to Start > Settings > Privacy. From here you can also separately define which apps can access the connected hardware like cameras and microphones etc.

9. How to Customize Battery Saver

The Windows 10 Battery Saver holds down on background activities in order to maximize your system's battery. You can also enable it from under Start > Settings > System > Battery Saver. It comes online spontaneously when the charge drops below 20%.

10. Unlock computer with a fingerprint

Windows 10 comprises of a suite of new biometric security features called Windows Hello. If you have the prerequisite hardware then you can use fingerprint detection or face recognition to *log in.*

GO to Start > Settings > Accounts > Sign-in options to discover the various available options.

11. Stream media through the network

Go to the 'Control Panel > Network and Internet > Network and Sharing Center' click on 'Change advance sharing settings'.

Now go to All Network section and click the 'Choose media streaming options' link and turn on media sharing.

12. Monitor with Task Manager

Windows 10 also contains an improved Task Manager with a well and improved layout and simply digestible information and useful graphs. Acquaint yourself with the Task Manager to monitor the resources of your computer and to terminate unresponsive processes.

13. To create a local account

If you don't need the benefits of OneDrive synchronised account, you can also create a separate offline account. Go to Start > Settings > Accounts and click the 'Sign in with a local account instead' link.

14. Contact Support

If you need any help from Microsoft contact setting up a Windows app or are facing any problems, you can use the Contact Support app under the Start > All apps menu.

15. Arrange windows 10

In addition to snap, you may arrange windows in other ways as well. Right-click on the taskbar to displays three window arrangement schemes: i.e., Cascade Windows, Show windows stacked, and Show windows side by side.

16. Scroll inactive windows 10

If you frequently work with multiple open

windows at the same time, Windows 10 allows you save time and effort by allowing you to scroll through inactive windows in the background when you hover over Windows.

17. Snap windows to corner

Windows 10 contains a Snap Assist feature which lets you snap two windows side-by-side by offering you an option of windows to snap. To snap a window to a quarter size of the monitor, just drag the window to a corner.

18. Use Virtual Desktops of Windows 10

Windows 10 lets you add multiple virtual desktops. To do this, click the Task View button on the taskbar and then click on new desktop button.

19. How to peek at the desktop

Right-click on the thin button at the far right end of the taskbar and select 'Peek at desktop'. Now when you roll the pointer over it, it'll show you a quick preview of the desktop and revert back when you move away from it.

20. View apps from across desktops

Normally, by default the taskbar displays windows and apps from the current desktop. To change this setting, Go to Start > Settings > System > Multi-tasking > Virtual Desktops and select the 'All desktops' option from your pull-down menu.

21. Move Windows between Virtual Desktops

To move windows between visual desktop, bring up the Task View and drag an open window from the current desktop straightforward into the desktop you need to move it into. Or drag a window to the 'new desktop' button in order to create a new virtual desktop for the window.

22. Get back icons on the desktop

For stress-free access to certain key locations on your PC, Go to Start > Settings > Personalization > Themes. Click 'Desktop icon Settings' and then select the icons you want to place on the desktop.

23. Manage your notifications

To customize which quick action icons are displayed in the Notification Center, Go to Start > Settings > System > Notifications and actions and then click on the four icons displayed to choice a different icon from a pull-down list.

24. Shake to minimize

To declutter your screen you can minimize all open windows except the one you're viewing currently. To do this just click, hold and shake its title bar. Repeat the action if you want to restore all minimized windows.

25. To enable jump lists

You can save great amount of time by using Jump Lists with the most used apps. Open the Settings app from Start Menu and go to Personalization > Start and enable the last option if you like to see jump lists on Start Menu and Taskbar.

26. To colorize Start

The default color of the Start Menu doesn't please all eyes especially after some hours of use. To pick your own color, Go to Start > Settings > Personalization > Colors and disable the 'Automatically pick an accent color from my background' option and pick an accent color from a palette.

27. How to Streamline Start

If you don't need Start Menu to display the most used programs in left-side pane, open Settings app from Start Menu and Go to Personalization > Start and set the 'Show most used apps' option to Off.

28. Hide recently opened apps

In the same way, if you don't want Start Menu to display your recently opened programs and files, head to Settings > Personalization > Start and toggle the 'Show recently added apps' option to off.

29. Select which folders appear on Start

Open the Settings app from Start Menu and go to Personalization > Start and click on the 'Choose which folders appear on Start' link. Now you can customize the folders list that shows on the Start menu.

30. Prevent an app from showing in the Recently Used List

You can prevent particular apps from showing up in the recently used apps list regardless of how frequently you use it instead of turning off the feature entirely.

To do this right-click on an app and select 'Don't show in this list'.

31. Operate keyboard-friendly Start

You can also operate the Start menu virtually using the keyboard. The Windows key to bring it as always and you can then use the search feature and the arrow keys to navigate it without any mouse.

32. Turn off Live Tiles

If you're preoccupied by the constant updates and changes in the tiles, you can turn off their ability to display updates. To do this just right-click on them and select the 'Turn live tile off' option.

33. Switch to Start Screen

If you want to pin more items to the Start menu you can really make it stretch across the entire screen. Go to Start > Settings > Personalization > Start and toggle the 'Use full-screen Start when in the desktop' option.

34. Pin most used settings

You can pin shortcuts, files and folders to Start Menu. To do this just right-click on the desired item and select the 'Pin to Start' option. This will directly pin the item to the right-side of Start Menu.

35. Change names and icons of the tiles

Simply, right-click on a tile of a non-Modern app then select the 'Open file location' option.

This will open the new Programs folder. Press F2 to rename the shortcut. To modify its icon, right-click on the shortcut and Go to Properties > Change Icon.

36. How to remove tiles

Alternatively, if you have no use for the tiles on the Start menu you can remove each and every one of them by right-clicking on each and selecting the 'Unpin from Start' option.

37. Resize the Start menu

To make more room for your customizations, you can simply resize the Start menu to your liking. Just move your mouse pointer to the top-border or right-border of the Start Menu, the pointer will change into an arrows and you'll be able to increase or decrease height and width.

38. Find apps faster

To shun scrolling through the alphabetically arranged list of apps, just click on any of the letters to view all the letters of the alphabet.

Then click any alphabet which takes you directly to the apps grouped below it.

39. Uninstall apps from the Start Menu

You can right-click on any New or a traditional desktop app in the Start menu and then select the 'Uninstall' option from the pop-up menu to remove that app from your computer.

40. Label and group tiles

In windows 10 default setting, the Start menu arranges tiles inside two groups. Click on these labels to rename them. If you've pinned tiles of your own, hover over the area above them and click on the two parallel lines to name the tiles group.

CHAPTER SIX

Windows 10 pro tips and tricks

41. Hide the task view button

If you don't use virtual desktops or use the keyboard to switch between them, you can be able to hide the Task View icon by right-clicking on the taskbar and deselecting the 'Show Task View button' option.

42. Remove Cortana's search box

Likewise, if you want to remove Cortana search box, you can reduce the space taken by Cortana in the taskbar. Just Right-click on an empty part of the taskbar, select Cortana and choose 'Hidden' to change it to a popup. You can keep Cortana on the taskbar as a standard icon by selecting the 'Show Cortana icon' option.

43. Find the original Control Panel in windows 10

The windows 10 new Settings panel is easy to find and is easier to navigate than the old Control Panel. But then again the latter is still available and comes in within reach for accessing advanced options. You can find it by pressing $Win + X$ on your keyboard and bringing up the power user menu.

44. Decrease effects

If you are running Windows 10 on a resource strapped device, you can squeeze extra performance by turning down the *bling. Go to Control Panel > System and Security > System and click 'Advanced system settings'. Then click Settings under the Performance section and customize the effects.*

45. Streamline the Navigation Pane

To streamline the Navigation Pane remove the OneDrive link in Windows Explorer launch the registry editor and head over to the key: HKEY_CLASSES_ROOT\CLSI D\ {018D5C66-4533-4307-9B53-224DE2ED1FE6}.

Now, in the right-side pane, modify the value of the System. IsPinned ToName

SpaceTree variable to 0.

46. Restore the previous Volume Control UI

To bring back the vertical volume lever in the system tray, just bring up the Registry Editor and head over to the HKEY_LOCAL_MACHINE\Software\Microsoft\Windows NT\CurrentVersion\ key. Then create a fresh key named MTCUVC and under it create a new DWORD named EnableMtcUvc and set its value to 0. The volume control UI will be restored.

47. Customize Quick Access

Quick Access permits you to jump into

your favorite folder and most recently used files. To customize its contents, switch to the View tab in Explorer and hit Options.

You should note that at the bottom of the General tab are further options to show or hide certain bits of information.

48. Customize the Power User menu

To reorganize and or remove entries go to C:\Users\\AppData\Local\Microsof t\Windows\WinX.

Here you'll see three folders that house entries for the Power User menu. You can move them around or remove them to suit your workflow.

49. Disable new battery flyout

To bring back the old battery display pattern in the taskbar, Go to the HKEY_LOCAL _MACHINE\Software \Microsoft\Windows \CurrentVersion\ImmersiveShell key in the Registry Editor.Here,you have to create a new DWORD named UseWin32BatteryFlyout and set its value to 1.

50. Make Cortana respond to all voice commands

If you want a hands-free operation, click on the Cortana search bar, select

Notebook from the left menu, choose Settings, and enable the 'Let Cortana respond to "Hey Cortana'" option.

Now repeat this phrase anytime to activate Cortana.

51. Make Cortana respond only to your voice command

You can ask Cortana to respond only to your voice. Go back to the Settings in the Notebook and press the 'Learn my voice' button and speak the phrases to teach Cortana your natural voice.

52. Cortana natural language search

Ever since Cortana can only understand natural language you can use it for complex search tasks. For instance, ask Cortana to 'Find pictures from May' 2019 and the intelligent assistant will dive through your local and online files and apply the proper filters to fetch results.

53. Share your preferences with Cortana

You can get better recommendations if you allow Cortana know your preferences. For instance, open Cortana's Notebook and Go to eat and drink to define your choice of cuisine, such as the price range and more. Now repeat this process for other sections as well.

54. Send an email with Cortana

You can use Cortana to send an email

hands-free. Say 'Send an email to [Kevin]' followed by the message. Cortana searches for the [Kevin] in the People app and composes the email with the text you spoke. If you don't like to make any changes, say 'Send'.

55. Cortana in Edge browser

The Cortana can also help you as you browse the Internet. To enable it in Microsoft Edge, Go to Settings > Advanced Settings >View Advanced Settings and under 'Privacy and Services' enable 'Have Cortana Assist Me in Microsoft Edge'.

56. Pin and reorder folders

You can pin folders in the Quick Access list on the navigation panel to make sure they don't disappear irrespective of their frequent or recent use. To adjust their listing order, just select a folder and drag it above or below the other listed folders.

57. Modification of the default view in File Explorer

File Explorer is the defaults to the Quick Access view, but if you want it to go straight to This computer on launch, click on the View tab, select Options and change the 'Open File Explorer to' setting to 'This PC'.

58. Selectively Sync folders with

OneDrive

Windows 10 OneDrive is now more flexible and user-friendly. To customize the folders it syncs, right-click on the OneDrive icon in the notification area, choice Settings, switch to the 'Choose folders' tab, and click the 'Choose folders' button to select the cloud folders that you need to be available locally.

60. How to automatically back up libraries

To back up your PC libraries, plug in an external drive and Go to Start > Settings > Update & Security > Backup.

Click on the 'Add a drive' option and

select the plugged in drive and enable the option, found under File History.

61. Access earlier versions of files

After you've set up the File History preference, you can also right-click on any file, select Properties, and open the Previous Versions tab to see former revisions to the file saved by either File History or Windows' system restore points.

62. Restart Explorer

To apply changes that require restarting the PC, launch the Task manager by right-clicking on the taskbar.

Click on 'More Details' button and

under the 'Processes' tab look for an entry named 'Windows Explorer'. Then right-click on it and select 'Restart'.

63. Change the location of Edge's Downloads folder

To force the Edge browser to use a custom Downloads folder, Go to the Registry Editor and navigate to HKEY_CURRENT_USER\SOFTWARE\Classes\Local Settings\Software\Microsoft\Windows\Current Version\AppContainer\Storage\microsoft.microsoftedge_8wekyb3d8bbwe\MicrosoftEdge\Main key.

Now create a new String named 'Default Download Directory' and set its value to the path of the new folder, such as D:\Downloads.

64. Swipe menu

All apps run full-screen when you're using Windows in the Tablet mode. To bring up the menu and access every commands and the window control, just swipe in from the top.

65. Analyze available storage space

To find out what kind of files are taking up more room on your PC, Go to Start > Settings > System > Storage and click on the drive name to get a breakdown of how the space is being used.

66. Save apps to external drives

If you want to use an SSD as your system drive you can ask Windows 10 to install apps on another disk by Go to Start > Settings > System > Storage and pointing to it under the 'New apps will save to' option.

67. Customize your default app associations

If the windows 10 default file associations don't work for you, you can change them by right-clicking on a file and selecting the 'Open with' option. Then select the 'Choose another app' option and pick the app you want to use.

69. Customize your app notifications

All Notifications from the installed apps can make you miss the real important ones. To limit notifications Go to Start > Settings > System > Notifications & action. Scroll down and selectively turn off apps that you don't want to hear from.

70. Offline maps

Offline maps save time and money when searching for directions on the go by downloading an offline version of a map. Go to Start > Settings > System > Offline Maps and click the Download maps button. Now you can also bit down to the geographic region you're interested in to download the map.

71. Side load Windows 10 apps

Windows 10 apps are like Android apps, Windows 10 now allows you install Windows apps from other sources besides the Windows Store. To enable this, simply Go to Start > Settings > Update & security > For developers and then click the 'Sideload app' option.

72. Speed up app launches on boot

On a super-fast device you can disable the artificial app startup delay. Launch regedit and navigate to HKEY_

CURRENT_USER\Software
\Microsoft\Windows\Current
Version\Explorer.

Right click Explorer, choice New > Key, and name it Serialize. Under this key, create a DWORD value called Startup DelayInMSec and set it to 0.

73. Run app as admin

If you want to run installed apps with escalated privileges for more autonomy, right-click on them and then select the 'Run as administrator' option. Remember that this capacity is available only for regular apps and isn't available for Recent apps.

74. Using the Power User menu

The new Start menu in Windows 10 doesn't bring back Control Panel to the menu list, but you've still got the power user menu from Windows 8. To do this, right-click on the Start icon or use the Win + X keyboard shortcut to bring it up.

75. How to Print to PDF document

You can save documents as PDFs without any third-party software as both the Current apps and the traditional desktop programs offer the option as part of their standard printing options.

76. Mail gestures

The new Mail app in Windows 10 supports a pair of gestures for common tasks. Click on the gears icon in the app to bring up the Settings and switch to Option section.

You can now enable the 'Swipe actions' option and use the pull-down menu to outline actions for the left and right swipe gestures.

77. To mount ISO images

If you want to mount ISO image, you don't need any third party software to browse the contents of an ISO image. Right-click on an ISO image and click 'Mount'.

The ISO images are auto-mounted as virtual discs and you can then access them from your PC File Explorer.

78. Manage contacts

A contact in the People app can contain an email address, work/home address and much more. And reliant on what information has been added to the contact, you can also use the app to launch a Map view of the address or compose an email to the contact.

79. Edge Reading improvement

Edge has a disturbance free view for reading web pages that you can switch to by clicking on the Reading View icon or pressing Ctrl + Shift + R on your PC keyboard

To configure the Reading View Go to Settings and scroll down to the Reading section.

80. Move Pictures from your phone

Plug your Android/iOS phone to your Windows 10 PC using the regular microUSB cable. This will quickly launch the new Phone Companion app with information about your phone.

Then scroll and select the 'Import photos and videos into the Photos app' option.

CHAPTER SEVEN

Windows 10 Prompt command

81. To enable new features in Command Prompt

The new Command Prompt in Windows 10 permits you to use Ctrl+C or Ctril+V to copy and paste commands more easily.

To activate this feature, just open the Command Prompt, right-click its title bar and select enable the new features under the 'Edit Options' section.

82. To record a video of an app

You can use Windows 10's Game DVR function to record your video of any open app or desktop software. Press Win + G to open the game bar which has a circular Record button. Recorded videos are saved under Video > Captures folder.

It is very important to note that recording may slow the performance depending on the demands of the app.

83. Edit and share photos

You can also use the built-in Photos app to fix several common photo flaws. You can straighten, sharpen, and apply filters effects on the images.

If you have already installed social apps

like Facebook or Twitter you can use Photos to share images with family and friends.

84. How to Generate a Battery Report

If you need to keep tabs on your laptops' battery level, launch the Administrative command prompt and type the following command: powercfg -energy -output C:\report.html. The command will analyze the battery status and then create a Power Efficiency Diagnostics Report in the root directory of the C: drive.

85. How to create a recovery disc

Plug in you USB drive and Go to Start > Settings and type 'recovery' in the Find a setting textbox and select the 'Create a recovery drive' option.

This will automatically launch a wizard which wipes the USB drive and transforms it into a recovery drive.

86. Create a system image

To create a system image, just Go to Start > Settings and type 'file' in the textbox and select the 'File History' tool. Then click the 'System Image Backup' link in the lower-left corner to start a wizard; this allows you select the destination drive for storing the backup image.

87. How to bypass the sign-in screen in

Windows 10

Speed up boot by logging into Windows 10 by typing 'netplwiz' in the search bar to bring up the User Accounts window.

In the Windows Users tab, deselect the 'Users must enter a username and password to use this computer' option.

88. How to set display per-monitor

With Windows 10 you can organize different DPI scaling ratios if you've got multiple monitors attached to your PC.

To do this, right-click on the desktop and Go to Display settings which lets you configure each detected display separately.

89. God mode of Windows 10

God Mode is a one-stop panel that collects all Control Panel commands within Windows 10. Create a folder on your desktop named: GodMode.{ED7BA470-8E54-465E-825C-99712043E01C}.

Once created the folder will modify to the Control Panel icon and rename itself 'GodMode'.

90. Customize Sync settings

You can simply take charge of the settings that synced from the current installation to your online account. Go over to Start > Settings > Accounts > Sync your settings and disable one of the listed settings that you don't want to sync with your Microsoft account.

91. Use maximum CPU power in Windows 10

Make sure you are using the maximum power of your main processor on a desktop computer running Windows 10 by going to Control Panel > Hardware and Sound > Power Options.

Then click Change Advanced Power settings > Processor power management > Minimum processor state and modify it to 100%.

92. Select no automatic updates

By default Windows 10 updates will

automatically restart your computer to finishing installing. To control that, Go to Start > Settings > Updates and Security > Windows Update > Advanced Options.

Under the 'Choose how updates are installed' pull-down menu, then select the 'Notify to schedule restart' option.

93. Schedule restarts

To remain working uninterrupted Windows 10, you can request Windows 10 to delay applying an update that needs a restart. Go to Start > Settings > Updates & security.

If you have an update pending, you can

re-schedule your reboot after selecting the 'Select a restart time' radio button.

94. Get updates from other sources

Windows 10 allows users to download updates from other PCs on the network and the Internet using peer-to-peer technology, relatively than Microsoft directly.

To tinker with the setting, Go to Settings > Update & Recovery > Windows Update > Advanced Options > Choose how you download updates.

95. Setup Metered connections

If you want to be connected with a mobile WiFi hotspot, you might configure it as a metered connection to restrict your data usage.

Go to Notifications > All settings > Network & Internet > WiFi > Advanced options and under 'Metered connection' enable the 'Set as metered connection' option.

96. Slide down the desktop to shutdown of Windows 10

Go to Windows > System32 bits and double-click on the slidetoshutdown.exe program. Execution this action from now on will drop in your lock screen image from the top and cover half of your screen.

Just slide the image to the bottom of your PC screen to shut down your computer.

97. Disable data collection in Windows 10

To prevent your PC from communicating with Microsoft HQ, type 'services' in the Start menu search bar to bring up the Services Management console. Find and disable the services named 'Diagnostics Tracking Service' and 'dmwappushsvc'. That is perfectly done.

98. Improved your Windows 10 Registry Editor

If you want to use the Registry Editor, Windows 10 lets you navigate the quintessential power user app with ease. You can jump between the same entries under the HKEY_LOCAL _MACHINE and HKEY_ CURRENT_ USER hives using a special context-menu entry.

99. How to modify Windows 10 update policy

If you want to constantly be notified of an impending Windows update, you can change the setting in the Registry Editor.

Launch regedit and Go to the HKEY_LOCAL_ MACHINE\SOFTWARE\Policies \Microsoft\Windows key. Now create a new key under Windows key and set its name as Windows Update.

Now create another new key under Windows Update key named AU. Then create a new DWORD named AU Options and set its value to 2. Finally click 'Check for updates' in Windows Update to bring the changes into effect.

100. To enable the handy Administrator account

Windows 10 by default, the built-in Administrator account is hidden to users. To enable it, launch the Command Prompt as Administrator and type net user administrator /active:yes.

At this time, logout to see the newly added Administrator account on the login screen.

101. Troubleshooting of windows 10

Select Start > Settings > Update & Security > Troubleshoot, or select the Find troubleshooters shortcut.

2. Select the type of troubleshooting you want to do, then select Run the troubleshooter.

3. Allow the troubleshooter to run and then answer any questions on the screen.

How to run Windows Troubleshooter?

1. Open Control Panel > Hardware and Sound > Configure a device.

2. On Windows 10, you can open Settings > Update & Security > Troubleshoot and click on Hardware and Devices.

3. The Hardware Troubleshooter will open. ...

4. Then Click on Next to run the Hardware and Devices Troubleshooter.

How to run diagnostics on Windows 10?

Generate your Windows 10 System Diagnostic Report

You should know that you need to be logged in as Administrator to run the report (which can also be generated on Windows 7). Just Hit Windows Key +

R on your keyboard to launch the Run dialog box and type: perfmon / report and hit Enter or click OK

How to fix your Windows 10 Start menu

As luck would have it, Windows 10 has a built-in way of resolving this.

1. Launch Task manager. ...

2. Run a new and fresh Windows task. ...

3. Run Windows PowerShell. ...

4. Run the System File Checker. ...

5. Reinstall Windows apps. ...

6. Launch Task manager. ...

7. Log into the new account. ...

8. Restart Windows in troubleshooting mode.

Why is your Windows 10 not updating?

If you are persistently receiving an error message with a specific error code, see Fix Windows Update errors to help resolve common update issues. Many updates often require you to restart your device. Save your work and close all open applications. Then, go to Start > Power , and choice either Update and restart or Update and shut down.

Why does start button not work on Windows 10?

Several problems with Windows come

down to corrupt files, and Start menu issues are no exception. To fix this, launch the Task Manager either by right-clicking on the taskbar and selecting Task Manager, or alternatively, hitting Ctrl+Alt+Delete. ... If this doesn't fix your Windows 10 Start menu issues, move on to the next option below

How to check for an errors in Windows 10?

1. Run the System File checker Tool

2. Login Windows 10.

3. Click the Search button on the bottom left side, and type command prompt

4. When you see the Command Prompt

program listed, then Right-click it, and click Run as administrator. ...

5. When the command prompt box comes up write the following then click Enter: sfc / scannow.

What to do when Windows 10 will not boot?

When Windows 10 Won't Boot? Fixes to Get Your PC Running Again

Try Windows Safe Mode. The weirdest fix for Windows 10 boot 1.

1. Problems is Safe Mode.

2. Check Your Battery.

3. Unplug All Your USB Devices.

4. Turn Off Fast Boot.

5. Try a Malware Scan.

6. Boot to the Command Prompt Interface.

7. Use System Restore or Startup Repair.

8. Reassign Your Drive Letter.

Conclusion

Thank you again for downloading this book!

I hope you have enjoyed this book and we hope that you are going to enjoy your Windows 10 excellently and efficiently. Finally, please take the time to share your thoughts and post a review on Amazon. It would greatly appreciate!

Thank you and good luck!

David H. Kevin is currently employed as a Senior Security Consultant for www.Techguideblog.net, before he worked with Software Ltd, a world-renowned security consultancy well known for its focus in enterprise-level application vulnerability research and database security. He has a background in Infrastructure and Information Security in a number of specialized environments such as financial services institutions, telecommunications companies, call centers, and other organizations across multiple continents. Kevin has experience in the integration of network infrastructure and telecommunications systems requiring high-caliber secure design, testing, and management. He has been involved in a variety of projects from the design and implementation of Internet banking systems to large-scale conferencing and telephony infrastructure, as well as penetration testing and other security assessments of business-critical infrastructure.

David H. Kevin

website is http//www.techguideblog.net

You should check it out and let me know

what you think. I keep a blog there for our efficient interaction. I like to invite you follow my journey, by signing up my free newsletter. If you subscribed you get free copy of my books.mp3, pdf files, and tutorials

Other book

Windows 10 (2019 edition)

The Ultimate user guide, How to master Windows 10 within 24 hours

It has been some years that Microsoft officially launched the latest version of windows 10 and we found out that a lot of people are delaying to upgrade not because they don't like the OS but because they are waiting for Microsoft to rectify some known issues. This book has come with solutions of your fears so you can enjoy this beast.

We identify how hard it is upgrading to a new operating system. They generally do not come with user manual and neither do genuine tutorials address the main issues. So, whether you have just upgraded from windows 8 to windows 10 or got a new PC that works with windows 10, there's an enormous probability that you're struggling with how things work. Performing simple tasks like taking security setting or how to personalize your desktop may become pretty confusing that you're so embarrassed to ask anyone.

In this book, we're going to be taking away what's old and bringing what's new. You will find out tips and tricks never featured on any blog post you've ever read. You will get a full introduction to windows 10 basics and outline the functionality of Cortana. To ensure your PC doesn't breakdown any time soon, we also outline safety tips and backup option for the longevity of your system.

This book features Simple but complex tips on how to perform actions on Windows 10. We take you through a step-by-step method with aid of screenshots on how to master the windows 10 interface from scratch to master's level.

Written in plain English that's easy to understand even for a 10 year old. We will take you from the windows 10 basic to the most advanced features.

Here is a preview of what you'll learn;

- *Windows 10 synopsis*

- *May 2019 Windows 10 update*

- *Installation of windows 10 (Upgrade and clean installs)*

- *Interaction with windows environment*

- *The Desktop setting*

- *Manage user Account setting*

- *Windows 10 updates and activation*

- *Cortana integrated in Microsoft Edge*

- *Windows 10 Troubleshooting*

And much more..!

Download your copy of "Windows 10" by scrolling up and clicking "Buy Now With 1-Click" button.

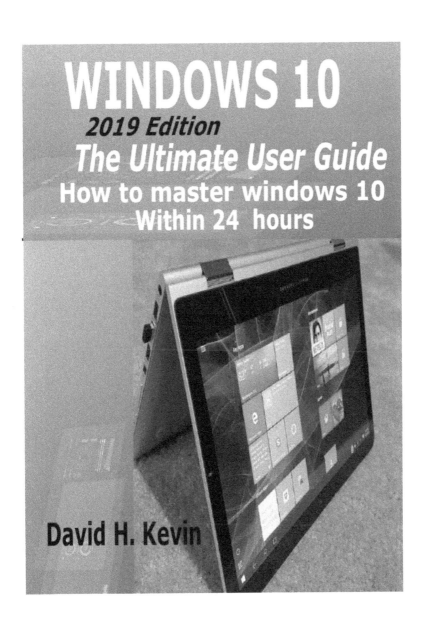

WINDOWS 10
2019 Edition
The Ultimate User Guide
How to master windows 10
Within 24 hours

David H. Kevin

www.ingramcontent.com/pod-product-compliance
Lightning Source LLC
Chambersburg PA
CBHW031240050326
40690CB00007B/888